BE A
MASTER ®
OF
SELF IMAGE

DR. KOUSOULI'S *33* MASTER SECRETS TO LIVING HEALTHIER, HAPPIER AND HOTTER

Dr. Theodoros Kousouli

A Personal Empowerment Book

Kousouli Enterprises
Los Angeles, CA

Heartfelt Gratitude to the following for their contributions:

Editing and research assistance: Latasha Doyle

Cover images of Dr. Kousouli and internal photography: Matthew A. Cooke

Cover couple image: Shutter Stock; ITALO

Layout coordinator: Gustavo Martinez

ISBN: 978-0997627626   Softcover
ISBN: 978-0997627633   Epub
ISBN: 978-0997627640   Kindle

Library of Congress Control Number: 2016909173

Kousouli Enterprises
P.O. Box 360494
Los Angeles, CA 90036

Printed in the United States of America

CONTENTS

Disclaimers vii

Introduction xi

Chapter One: How Our Relationship to Food Has Changed 1

➣ History of Fasting and Food 2

➣ Eating Now 2

➣ Defining "Fat" 3

➣ Interesting Facts About Obesity 4

➣ How Western Culture "Treats" Obesity 4

➣ Prescription Drugs 5

➣ Risky and Costly Surgery 6

Chapter Two: Cleansing Mind and Spirit 7

➣ Prayer and Meditation 7

➣ Obesity and Depression 8

➣ *Secret Fit Tip #1: HAVE A SUPPORT GROUP HANDY* 9

➣ Addressing Negativity to Improve Health 9

Chapter Three: It's Not Just the Food You Eat 11

➣ *Secret Fit Tip #2: TRY HYPNOSIS FOR WEIGHT LOSS* 11

➣ *Secret Fit Tip #3: RESEARCH HORMONE REPLACEMENT* 12

➣ *Secret Fit Tip #4: GET CHIROPRACTIC ADJUSTMENTS*
REGULARLY 13

➣ *Secret Fit Tip #5: DO TOILET ABDOMINAL MASSAGE DAILY* 14

Chapter Four: The Importance of Gut Health 17

➣ *Secret Fit Tip #6: PAY ATTENTION TO GUT MOVEMENT; ADD*
FIBER 18

➣ *Secret Fit Tip #7: TAKE PROBIOTICS DAILY & USE DIGESTIVE*
ENZYMES WITH EACH MEAL 19

➣ *Secret Fit Tip #8: CHEW YOUR FOOD WELL BEFORE*
SWALLOWING 20

Chapter Five: Food Is Like Friends – Pick the Right Ones 23

➤ *Secret Fit Tip #9: CUT OUT REFINED WHEAT AND SUGAR* 23

➤ *Secret Fit Tip #10: DROP MEAT, GO PLANT BASED* 24

➤ *Secret Fit Tip #11: USE PLANT PROTEIN POWDER TO FILL UP HEALTHY & FAST.* 25

➤ *Secret Fit Tip #12: DRINK CHIA SEEDS TO FEEL FULL* 26

➤ *Secret Fit Tip #13: DRINK APPLE CIDER VINEGAR + RAW MANUKA HONEY & CINNAMON* 26

➤ *Secret Fit Tip #14: USE DRIED FRUIT AS YOUR NEW GO-TO SNACK.* 27

➤ *Secret Fit Tip #15: WATCH WHAT YOU DRINK* 27

➤ *Secret Fit Tip #16: DROP THE SALT* 29

➤ *Secret Fit Tip #17: HOT PEPPERS AND SPICES HELP TURN UP METABOLISM* 29

➤ *Secret Fit Tip #18: ADD PSYLLIUM HUSKS TO YOUR DAILY DIET* 30

Chapter Six: Addressing it All; Spirit, Body, and Mind 31

➤ Staying in the Positive Cycle 35

➤ Reverting Back to the Negative Cycle through Neglect. 36

Chapter Seven: Detoxification 39

➤ *Secret Fit Tip #19: ONE WEEK FAST EACH SEASON* 39

➤ Removal of the "Acid State" 40

➤ *Secret Fit Tip #20: DETOX THE BLOOD AND DIGESTIVE TRACT.* 41

➤ Benefiting From a Good Colon Cleansing Program 41

➤ Detox with Caution 42

➤ What to Expect From a Detox 42

➤ Cleansing by Chelation Therapy. 43

Chapter Eight: It's Not About the Numbers! 45

➤ *Secret Fit Tip #21: STOP COUNTING* 45

➤ *Secret Fit Tip #22: HIDE THE SCALE* 46

➤ *Secret Fit Tip #23: UNDERSTAND RESTING METABOLISM.* 47

Chapter Nine: Tips to Trick Your Brain into Making Healthy Choices 49

➤ *Secret Fit Tip #24: DON'T ADD EXTRAS TO THE MEAL; GO LIGHT* 49

➤ *Secret Fit Tip #25: COOK AT HOME; EAT OUT LESS.* 50

➤ *Secret Fit Tip #26: REMOVE ALL DISTRACTIONS WHILE EATING.* 50

➤ *Secret Fit Tip #27: SLEEP FOR BETTER HORMONE METABOLISM* 51

➤ *Secret Fit Tip #28: BRUSH YOUR TEETH AFTER DINNER* 52

➤ *Secret Fit Tip #29: USE IMAGING PROGRAMS TO YOUR BENEFIT* 52

Chapter Ten: Exercise for Total Body Health. 55

➤ *Secret Fit Tip #30: STRETCH DAILY* 55

➤ Kousouli® Spinal Stretches (KSS®) 57

➤ Benefits to the KSS® Stretch Program 63

➤ *Secret Fit Tip #31: 30 MINUTES OF AEROBIC EXERCISE DAILY* .. 64

➤ *Secret Fit Tip #32: TAKE MORNING JOGS AND EVENING WALKS* 64

Chapter Eleven: Adding Supplements to Support Weight Loss 67

➤ *Secret Fit Tip #33: TRY NATURAL SUPPLEMENTS FOR WEIGHT LOSS* 68

Chapter Twelve: Conclusion. 71

About the Author 73

Be a Master® of Self Image

BE A MASTER® OF MAXIMUM HEALING
How to Lead a Healthy Life Without Limits

- Holistics Solutions for over 60 Diseases to Help You and Your Loved Ones Heal!

BE A MASTER® OF PSYCHIC ENERGY
Your Key to Truly Mastering Your Personal Power

- Uncover and Amplify Your Hidden Psychic Abilities to Change Your Life!

BE A MASTER® OF SEX ENERGY
Hypnotize Your Partner for Love and Great Sex

- Build a Stronger Bond with Your Lover(s) Using Subconcious Science!

BE A MASTER® OF SUCCESS
Dr.Kousouli's 33 Master Secrets to Achieving Your Dreams

- Solid Success Principles You can Apply to Empower Your Life!

BE A MASTER® OF SELF LOVE
Dr.Kousouli's 33 Master Secrets to Loving Your Extraordinary Life

- Overcome Bullying, Abuse, Depression and Build Massive Self-Esteem & Self-Love!

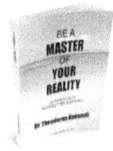

BE A MASTER® OF YOUR REALITY
Authentically Manifest Your Desires

- Use the Law of Attraction to Radically Transform Your Life!

DISCLAIMER

In a land where being politically correct seems more 'right' than standing for the 'truth,' or more desired than expressing an honest opinion, it's sad that I must digress and add the following legal disclaimer to remind you, the reader, that *you must think for yourself.*

This book is a collection of experiences and research that form my thoughts, opinions, and conclusions as a board certified Doctor of Chiropractic (D.C.) and Hypnotherapist (CHt); not a Doctor of Medicine (M.D.). The content herein is controversial as it presents an alternative view to the status quo. There are establishments who may disagree with certain contents of this book, and would have preferred that this information never found your eyes. However, this book is not intended for them; it was written for the countless individuals yearning for better health and well-being amongst a society that has lost its way.

The writings in this book are based on my personal research, experience, interpretations and beliefs. Your personal beliefs will affect your ability to review this material, as you will put it through your own filters. I intend to guide you in developing your own ability to use your personal energy in a healthy manner, and this book is a guide for you to grow, but is not by any means the final word on the subject.

I encourage you, the reader, to research, analyze and develop your own opinions on the subject matters discussed. As a holistic health care provider, I express the truth as I have come to know it. It is my duty to aid in the growth of my beloved patients, family, and friends with this love so they, too, may reach the heights of what their Creator made possible for them to be.

Theodoros Kousouli D.C., CHt

LEGAL DISCLAIMER

This book is dedicated to my lovely patients and their growth that I have witnessed through the years. I am honored to be your advisor and confidant through both challenge and triumph. May God continue to bless each and every one of you in the unveiling of your life's work.

❖ ❖ ❖

"The life so short, the craft so long to learn."
~ Hippocrates

IN THIS BOOK, YOU WILL LEARN:

- ✓ How to take natural approaches to regulating your weight, and how to get "Hollywood skinny" without ruining your body or your mind.

- ✓ How the lies we are told about our bodies affect our opinion of ourselves. When we hold a negative view of ourselves, our health decreases.

- ✓ How to debunk the myths of dieting and calorie counting, and how to deflect the enticement of plastic surgery in today's society.

- ✓ How to break old habits and instill new ones using hypnosis so you can change your mindset and lifestyle for the long run.

- ✓ How negative emotions keep you from the weight and body you've always wanted, and how to work through those emotions to come to an all-around healthier you.

- ✓ How your nervous system plays a big part in losing weight, gaining health, and living a long life.

- ✓ How to maximize your body's potential through detoxification, and what you can do to keep toxins out.

- ✓ And so much more....

Introduction

*"That lying little voice inside your head; the one that whispers against
that which your higher-self knows better, is jealous of
how incredible you can become."*

~ *Dr. Theo Kousouli*

It seems like we are getting input on our appearance, our beauty, our
weight, and our overall looks from every direction – and we are! TV
tells us that these women are beautiful and thin, those men are fit
and handsome, but *you* don't look like that. Marketing tells women
that in order to be loved and happy, they have to buy this latest shade
of lipstick, and men have to use this new soap or body spray.

But the most insidious of these messages is the idea that people
can forgive pretty much anything, as long as you're not fat. We insult
people's weight, the food they eat, the way they look in clothes, more
than we insult them for anything else. In our society, we'd rather be
unhappy than "fat." This is a sad, sad state of affairs, and one that
affects *all* of us, not just the ones who publicly struggle with weight.

This approach to our health and our obsession with being "Hollywood skinny" affects our children, as well as teens, adults, and *everyone* as they age. As a practitioner working just outside of Hollywood, and in the heart of Beverly Hills, I see this all the time with
my clients.

"Dr. Kousouli, I can't seem to lose this weight, I'm so unhappy,
I feel so fat." I hear these things all the time. These thoughts are not
serving us, and the messages we are attacked with daily are making
it worse. But when I was asked to write a book on fitness and weight
loss, I cringed.

I know the last thing people need is another one of those calorie crunching, fad diet types of books that collect on the bookshelf,

along with the countless hype marketing fitness books pandering to the desperate public. If I was going to write about health and fitness, I wanted to tell you the truth.

This book is going to serve as your awakening, to show you that your weight struggles and lack of confidence all stem from your negative relationship to societal inputs and to food. This book will show you different ways you can make yourself healthy *without* taking the latest fad diet pill or paying an arm and a leg for liposuction. You will have the tools you need to be happy, healthy, and "Hollywood skinny" in your own right.

Chapter One:
How Our Relationship to Food Has Changed

"Take care of your body. It's the only place you have to live."

~ Jim Rohn

We all know that cavemen used to hunt for meat and forage for berries and greens, and the struggle to always find food kept humans motivated to stay alive for millennia. Now, we look around and we have more food in one week than some people have in a whole month in some places around the world.

But scientists believe that our "struggle to survive" and hoarding mentality with food has been ingrained in our DNA for the long haul. Our species had to eat when food was available, and try to sustain themselves through the times when there was none. This scarcity mentality may or may not drive our need to overeat, but it does explain why we love to binge on food when it's in front of us.

But once we realize that we've had an unhealthy relationship with food, we pack up and head the other direction: towards dieting, "fasting," and doing whatever we can to shed those extra pounds. Either way we look at it, we have this scarcity mindset - not enough food, not skinny enough, and so on. Instead of understanding this attachment to food and how it changes our bodies, we have developed a disrespect of food and instead abuse our bodies for not looking the way we want.

To reverse this, we have to evaluate how this relationship evolved, and understand how our relationship with food and our bodies *used* to be, in an effort to return to our body's natural inclination towards health.

History of Fasting and Food

Not even a century ago, men and women who were "plumper" were considered healthier, wealthier, and happier because they obviously had the resources to purchase food. Women with a few extra pounds were considered beautiful and desirable because they were not frail, would bear children easier, and didn't get sick often.

Not only that, but up until about the 1920's and '30's, food was purchased and eaten fresh because we didn't have the resources to flash-freeze, can, or factory-make food that could sit on the shelves for months at a time. Introducing all of these new foods and concoctions has been connected to the increase in obesity and health issues in thousands of studies over a number of decades, the most largest of which came from the Centers for Disease Control in 2009.

Religious approaches to food, especially, have been overlooked in recent years. Food was actually rationed and used in religious practices or places of worship to make sure people had food to eat; not too much, but enough. This is why fasting holidays like Ramadan, Lent, Yom Kippur, and others were supported through the years; it not only kept food rationed but it also kept religious practitioner's bodies clean. This is why some Christians and most Jewish followers consider pork "unclean" to this day, and why meats and grains are often reserved for celebration and religious feasts. Religions have long held a better relationship to food and nature than humans have had on their own.

Eating Now

After working for over a decade in Beverly Hills, I have had the honor and privilege of working with many amazing souls who look to discover and express their innate gifts to reach the world stage. Sadly, an important aspect of succeeding in our society is possessing the singular type of body or beauty that "everyone" says is best.

To get these types of bodies, people stop eating, only eat select few things, take dangerous diet pills, binge and purge, and generally forget that food is something that should honor our body. We start to disregard how food nourishes and heals us, and instead we look at it like something that is trying to "make us fat." If we think of it this way, the law of attraction will bring us more of what we are thinking, and the fat will continue to pack on. In manifestation, "like attracts like," and so on.

Now, there are the latest fad diets, new "super foods" every week, and people are constantly falling off and jumping back on the bandwagon to gain muscle and lose fat. (How's that New Years Resolution going, by the way?) But we don't really know what our bodies are capable of, and we assume that everything that doesn't look like what we see in those TV commercials and magazines is inherently bad.

Defining "Fat"

We can't go a day without hearing "She's fat," or "I feel so fat," or "I'm getting fat, I need to start working out," and odds are we say the same things about and to ourselves. But let's make some clear definitions here, so we have a starting point for all future discussions of "fat."

Obesity is caused by abnormal fat, or adipose tissue deposition in the body. It is mostly caused by a sedentary lifestyle and bad dietary habits. Obesity may also be a symptom of other underlying disease conditions, like thyroid problems or Type I or II Diabetes.

Being overweight or obese is very common, with about 35% of all Americans qualifying as overweight or obese. But it's not the just total sum of our waistlines at risk here; it's our overall health. Being overweight has serious life threatening consequences and can lead to stroke, high blood pressure, sleep apnea, libido and reproductive issues, Type II diabetes, heart disease, gallbladder disease, pancreatic, endometrial, colon, and breast cancers, damage to joints and bones, scoliosis, respiratory issues, decreased oxygen, cognitive impairments... just to name a few.

Interesting Facts About Obesity

Europeans are generally less obese than their American counterparts. Also, if you travel and visit indigenous cultures you won't find the obesity problem we have here in America. Simply put, you can't gain weight if you are constantly moving around because you consume the energy you have stored. In America, and in countries whose foods have become 'Americanized' (processed), we see larger and larger waistlines due to inactivity or little to no movement lifestyles.

In the West, we consume more chemically processed foods than any other areas in the world, and we eat high calorie and fried foods nearly every day! Unlike indigenous cultures and even people in Europe or the East, we're not catching our own food or even cooking it ourselves. We get into our cars, arrive at the supermarket, choose our boxed nutrient deficient food, and drive back to our kitchens where we let a microwave nuke the "food" so we can eat. Worse yet, we just drive through the fast food chain's drive-thru and spend money clogging our arteries buying dollar menu items that can't possibly be actual food. There is no way to spend less money buying 'real' food than it costs for the company to prepare the other mystery 'stuff'!

We're so "tired" from our pressures to produce money to pay for our gadget-filled, convenient lifestyles that we don't even go to the gym to work off the pounds. In the end, we end up with diseases, doctor visits, and seek sympathy and medication for our misfortune. But the issue is more between our ears than it is between our hips.

How Western Culture "Treats" Obesity

After serving in the holistic health care arena for over a decade, I know there's no doubt about it - Americans are trapped on their prescription pills. Did you know that Big Pharma generates over $300 billion in sales *each year* in the United States? Companies that market prescription weight loss drugs report double or triple earnings just in their first year of release - making these companies millions of dollars because they tell people their drug is "the miracle weight loss cure" they've been looking for.

Like most of the medical industrial complex, **too many weight loss drugs are given out like candy.** When prescription or over-the-counter weight loss pills don't work, many people resort to surgery. It's a personal choice, but I ask that you enlist the help of a plastic surgeon only when all other natural options have been exhausted. Natural is safer and cheaper!

While drugs and surgery may seem like valid (and fast) options, especially when your trusted doctors are recommending them, it's important to understand how these options work, and what you can expect from them. These are a few of the medications and procedures doctors recommend:

Prescription Drugs

Used for weight control; when medication is stopped, the weight returns. Side effects are very common.

- *Orlistat (Xenical):* Blocks digestion and absorption of fat. Side effects may include: Frequent oily bowel movements, urgency, and gas.

- *Phentermine, (Suprenza, Adipex-P), Phentermine-topiramate (Qsymia):* Appetite suppressants. Side effects may include: Hand and foot tingling, insomnia, dizziness, dry mouth, constipation, increased heart rate, suicidal thoughts, mood changes, problems with memory or comprehension, sleep disorders, and changes to vision, or passing out - just to name a few.

- *Lorcaserin (Belviq):* Affects chemicals in your brain that decrease your appetite and make you feel full.

Risky and Costly Surgery

- *Gastrointestinal Bypass:* Risky and invasive. Long recovery period.

- *Laparoscopic Adjustable Gastric Banding (LAGB):* Less invasive, therefore the most popular. Shorter recovery period with very specific dietary restriction for up to a year afterwards.

- *Gastric Sleeve:* Surgery where some of the stomach is removed, creating a smaller pocket for food.

- *Biliopancreatic Diversion with Duodenal Switch:* Most of the stomach is surgically removed; greater risk of vitamin deficiency and malnutrition. Long recovery period.

- **Laser Liposuction:** A much more advanced and safer way to remove subcutaneous fat (the fat you can pinch), with minimal scarring and bruising. Cost ranges from $5 to 10+ grand. Minimal recovery period, but fat may return if you don't change your lifestyle.

Essentially, this whole chapter has been targeted at highlighted the *real* problem we have with food. Food is not inherently evil; it's not "out to get you." Our society's relationship to food, and pretty much everything we value over our health and our bodies, affects us. Once we understand those external influences, it's easier then to work on ourselves.

Chapter Two:
Cleansing Mind and Spirit

*"Feelings are real. They often become one's reality. But they
are not always based on truth."*

~ *Jesikah Sundin*

As a passionate holistic practitioner, energy healer, and hypno-
tist, I *know* that diets and all those weight loss products just
don't work. Why? Because they don't address the real issues at hand;
why you've gained weight or have developed an unhealthy relationship with food in the first place. I firmly believe that, in order to
cleanse the body, you have to cleanse your mind and spirit, too.

Prayer and Meditation

If you are religious, attend ceremonies at your church or place of
worship, and pray frequently, this can be a powerful tool in helping
you create the life, health, and body you've always wanted. Accepting
that there is a higher power at work that can help you overcome your
struggles is incredibly uplifting, and can give you the boost you need
to get started and/or keep going.

Prayer is useful in cases where you've developed unhealthy habits, anywhere from overeating to anorexia or emotional eating. Simply praying for support, and surrendering full control can start the
healing process. Knowing you're not alone is immeasurably powerful in this (and any) battle.

Meditation is an incredibly valuable tool in your weight loss and
healthy lifestyle arsenal. If you're not familiar with meditation, try
to erase the preconceived notion you have of a monk sitting on a
mountain top. What meditation actually involves is *mindful aware-*

ness. You give yourself the ability to view your thoughts and emotions without acting upon them, without judging them; just being *aware of them.*

Cultivating this ability alone can change a number of dynamics in your life, from your need to be busy, to your inability to be alone with yourself. These negative emotions and thoughts all affect your relationship with yourself, which means that you do not treat your body as the temple that it actually is.

Meditation can also help you visualize the life and body you want, and can give you the insights you need to address your "inner demons." Without reflecting on yourself, without taking time to become aware of your thoughts, you're not going to properly approach your weight loss efforts.

Although meditation and prayer are very important in developing the right mindset, proper action must also be taken - especially intuitive action. For help in developing your intuition for guided action, read my previous book, *BE A MASTER® OF PSYCHIC ENERGY,* which will help guide you in the steps of proper meditation and prayer.

Obesity and Depression

In 2010, the CDC released their Census report on the connections between obesity and depression. 43% of all adults diagnosed with depression were obese, and obese adults were statistically more likely to be mildly to severely depressed than their thinner counterparts. You probably know how obesity affects mental health; many people know the struggle to overcome their weight issues.

This is a lot like the "chicken and the egg" argument, though. Does depression cause obesity, or does obesity cause depression? It's most likely different for everyone, but the reality is that, in order to reach a fully happy, healthy life, you have to address the mental health concerns that are attached to your relationship with your body and/or food. I address the issues of depression, self love, and happiness in my book *BE A MASTER® OF SELF LOVE.*

> ## Dr. Kousouli's Secret Fit Tip #1
> ## HAVE A SUPPORT GROUP HANDY

Because getting fit also involves addressing your emotional history, having a support group can really change the game. Support groups can come in any form – whether it's your family, friends, or people who are struggling with the same issues.

Support is also helpful if you're struggling with mental health concerns, or are concerned that you may have an eating disorder. For help with these issues, please reach out to professionals and support groups in your area:

- National Eating Disorder Association: http://www.nationaleatingdisorders.org/find-help-support 1-800-931-2237
- Obesity Support Groups (online forum) http://obesity.supportgroups.com
- National Suicide Prevention Lifeline: 1-800-273-8255
- Anxiety and Depression Association of America: http://www.adaa.org/finding-help

Addressing Negativity to Improve Health

We are all familiar with at least some sort of negativity surrounding our appearance, our health, and our happiness. "I look terrible," or "I feel fat in this dress," or "I don't look good at all." We're all guilty of these self-talks, but you should know that this doesn't serve you. By addressing the negative thoughts and emotions you have that center on yourself or food, you can address your weight and self-image concerns much easier.

There are also concerns with other environmental factors affecting your health, including your work environment, stress load, etc. Any kind of negative emotion can use up reserve energy, tax body function, increase free radicals, and create acidity. An increase in stress beyond normal amounts can lead to acidosis (an over-accumulation of acid in the body). Have you ever heard the saying, "I am sick to my stomach"? or "Your problems are eating away at your happiness?" These statements reflect emotional states, which make you highly prone to acidosis and set the stage for dis-ease.

Chapter Three:
It's Not Just the Food You Eat

*"If you don't do what's best for your body, you're the one
who comes up on the short end."*
~ Julius Erving

I have heard it time and time again: "Dr. Kousouli, I've tried x/y/z diet and I work out a lot, but I can't seem to lose these pounds!" It can be incredibly frustrating when you aren't seeing results when you think you're using all the right resources to make a difference.

In this chapter, we're going to discuss why you *need* to address other issues within your body before you can lose weight. Many people don't understand the importance of their nervous or digestive systems in the weight loss and health improvement process. Let's dip into this a little bit.

> ### Dr. Kousouli's Secret Fit Tip #2
> ### TRY HYPNOSIS FOR WEIGHT LOSS

Addictions don't just come in the form of illicit drugs or alcohol. Many, many people in today's fast food society are addicting to sugar, caffeine, and heavy-duty carbs. If you don't think you can be addicted to those substances, try quitting them cold-turkey. You'll have classic withdrawal symptoms, like fever, aches, stomach issues, excess sweating, pain and more. These are normal indications of withdrawal, and although they are signs that your body is moving towards healing, many succumb to their symptoms and allow the cravings to take over again.

Cutting out the junk food from your diet is way harder than most of us think. In order to circumvent the struggle, I often recommend hypnosis for weight loss, sugar detox, and food triggers for my clients. However, not all hypnosis CD's or hypnosis coaches can get everyone the success they seek. A qualified hypnotherapist knows when the patient is ready for hypnosis and how the hypnosis must be performed.

Many times, 'layering' of new subconscious programming over several sessions is needed to achieve a deeper longer lasting effect. A general shotgun approach may work with some people who are easily suggestible, but I find general hypnosis templates to be a waste of time that cause the uneducated public to unhappily claim that "hypnosis doesn't work."

My success stems from the extra time it takes me to personalize the session through various proprietary methods of attack for maximum results. A therapist must not only have the correct credentialing, but more importantly they must have the prior experience and deep desire to do the tedious detective work (along with the patient's relentless determination to be involved in their own healing) to reverse the deep subconscious programming that keeps the patient from reaching their max potential.

Of note; it is also not uncommon that in regression hypnotherapy sessions, we uncover problems with food in previous life incarnations, which have continued on and need to be dealt with in the present day. These sessions tend to be miraculous in nature when the actual cause and effect of the issue is addressed from a spiritual level and brought into a physical manifestation.

Dr. Kousouli's Secret Fit Tip #3
RESEARCH HORMONE REPLACEMENT

Women often struggle with their weight more than men because of their hormone levels. Fluctuations in monthly hormone levels can lead to water retention, weight gain, etc., while events like meno-pause can entirely change metabolism because a woman's hormones are entirely changing throughout her life.

As men age, they also experience hormone fluctuations with tes-tosterone, and they struggle with burning fat like they could when they were younger. These aren't just "excuses" for weight gain; they're real! A lot of nutritionists and whole health practitioners focus on hormones as a direct cause to obesity and weight struggles, and test-ing can be done to make sure you don't have thyroid hormone issues as well.

There are plenty of natural solutions for hormone deficiencies, varying from eating more healthy oils (coconut oil, avocado, Ome-ga-3 rich fish, etc.), to focusing on sleep and cutting out caffeine. There are herbs and supplements that can be taken, as well. I recom-mend that you talk to your holistic practitioner, nutritionist, naturo-path, or integrative medicine doctor (who specialize in a healing-ori-ented practice and take into account the 'whole person') about your hormone levels, and then developing a supplement or diet regimen that can help return your levels to your "normal."

Dr. Kousouli's Secret Fit Tip #4
GET CHIROPRACTIC ADJUSTMENTS REGULARLY

What many overweight people don't know is that there may be a spinal connection and nerve interference issue in the digestive and intestinal systems which may cause sluggish function, thus contrib-uting to acidosis, toxic buildup, and more weight. Your whole body is affected by your nervous system's ability to put out the proper in-structional signals, and if your nerves aren't able to communicate with the rest of your body, nothing works like it should; especially re-moving toxic waste. Ask your Chiropractor about adjusting Occiput, C1, C2 and the associated gastrointestinal spinal areas, as well as the

T5-S5 / coccygeal spinal levels. Obviously, these won't mean much to you, but your Chiropractor will know exactly what I'm talking about. These areas in your spine directly communicate with the stomach, liver, small and large intestines, rectum, and colon. Adjusting these areas (over the course of a proper care plan) helps keep gut communication in top shape and rules out sluggish nerve function. Adjustments may even help with constipation and some food sensitivities. Patients who haven't gone to the bathroom and come in for spinal adjustment are astonished that they can actually start again to eliminate and become "regular" right after treatment. Spinal adjustments will also improve your respiration and oxygen intake, thus contributing to boost your alkalinity, preventing acidosis and dis-ease! The spine and nervous system has immense power in it; treat them right!

Dr. Kousouli's Secret Fit Tip #5
DO TOILET ABDOMINAL MASSAGE DAILY

How many times have you heard that there is a right and wrong way to eliminate your bowels? Probably not often, but it's the truth. Without the proper squatting posture, and without an abdominal massage, waste can remain in your lower intestine and rectum, which leads to decreased gut health and waste elimination.

To fix this, every time you are on the toilet, your intestines can greatly benefit from a daily abdominal self-massage. When you are sitting on the toilet to have a bowel movement, place your feet on a telephone book while seated to get more into a squatting position. This will help you eliminate more fecal matter. While going sit up straight and lean slightly back; breathe deeply from the diaphragm (not the chest). Use a clockwise motion with your right hand in a fist; massage your front abdominal area in a clockwise motion. At the same time, use your left hand's palm or fingers to stroke straight down the back of your spine. This encourages peristaltic movement of waste through the intestines.

You should also consider ten or more sessions with a Rolfing therapist who performs deep organ massage that can help break up adhesions in the deep viscera. This greatly improves organ function and intestinal flow. When your body properly eliminates, you have improved health and can lose weight faster. In the next chapter, we discuss gut health in depth.

Chapter Four:
The Importance Of Gut Health

"If there's one thing to know about the human body; it's this: the human body has a ringmaster. This ringmaster controls your digestion, your immunity, your brain, your weight, your health and even your happiness. This ringmaster is the gut."
~ Nancy S. Mure

Disregarding our gut health is something that we are all guilty of at some point or another. We often get frustrated with our digestive systems when it can't handle the delicious fried foods or excessive amount of alcohol we consumed last night. But if you're really serious about getting "Hollywood skinny" without causing yourself further damage, take a good long look at your gut health.

In our guts, we have approximately one hundred trillion strains of bacteria that line our tract's insides. Now, bacteria can be good or bad; you should aim for more good bacteria (obviously). The foods we eat change the bacterial makeup of our stomachs, pushing the bacteria to the "dark side" if we eat too much junk. Foods like sauerkraut, kefir, kombacha, kimchi and Greek yogurt can help us heal our gut.

About 85% of our fat is subcutaneous (under the skin), the stuff we can pinch with our fingers. The remaining 15% is deep fat, called visceral intra-abdominal fat, is under the abdominal wall and not pinch-able.

Fat sheets, called the greater and lesser omentum, are covered by a serous membrane that lines the abdomen cavity and covers the organs (called a peritoneum). In order to really lose weight, you have to address gut and omentum health. Poor food choices lead to bad bacteria levels increasing, and our body literally treats this as an attack. It reacts with an immune response, triggering indigestion and even inflamed joints, skin rashes, overall body pain and more.

Chronic inflammation like this is what causes dis-ease; cancer, asthma, allergies, diabetes, and pretty much any other condition you can think of can be affected by (and arguably – caused by) our gut health. It's time to start building better gut health so you can have the body you've always wanted, and so that your body can last longer. Pay attention to your gut.

Dr. Kousouli's Secret Fit Tip #6
PAY ATTENTION TO GUT MOVEMENT; ADD FIBER

In an article published by Scientific American in March 2015, people with low amounts of fiber had more "bad" bacteria and less "good" bacteria in their guts. This eventually correlates to more belly fat, more obesity, and less overall health (dis-ease). People who ate at least 21 grams of fiber a day reported easy weight loss, and they kept the weight off as long as they kept up the fiber intake. Fiber helps move food along, and increases normal defecation. As a general rule: if you have three meals, you should be eliminating three times that day. If you eat three large meals and go to the bathroom once every other day, where are those meals going? They're packing in your intestines and colon!

If you really want to lose weight, stop thinking about how to count calories and focus on what you're putting IN and what's coming OUT of your body. It's not all about how much sugar or how many carbs there are in something – look at the fiber. And don't just eat fiber bars and junk with "Fiber Added!" plastered on the label. Eat natural foods that are rich in fiber, including: berries, quinoa, peas, lentils, mung beans, spinach, almonds (and other nuts), squash, cauliflower, broccoli, avocado, and more.

Dr. Kousouli's Secret Fit Tip #7
TAKE PROBIOTICS DAILY & USE DIGESTIVE
ENZYMES WITH EACH MEAL

You've probably heard (or tried) a few probiotics because you've heard how awesome they are for your digestion. If you have stomach, digestion issues, irritable bowel syndrome, leaky gut syndrome, a gluten intolerance, etc., probiotics can be a total game changer.

But what most people don't know is that probiotics work to change the overall environment within your gut, balancing the good bacteria in your favor. As mentioned before, people who are in a high state of acidosis or dis-ease have too much "bad" bacteria in their systems, which prevents foods from properly digesting and being absorbed and used by the body.

Authority Nutrition published an article in April 2016 that reviews all of the findings surrounding probiotic use in weight loss. It has been found that probiotics actually help the body release more of the peptide hormone that makes us feel full (so we eat less), and patients who took lactobacillus strains experienced 50% more weight loss than patients who took nothing.

Other findings published in the *Therapeutic Advances in Gastroenterology* journal indicate that many doctors and professionals are prescribing probiotics to their patients because they dramatically improve conditions like: diarrhea, ulcerative colitis, Crohn's disease, leaky gut, and irritable bowel syndrome.

To get the most out of a probiotic, take one with a high strain count over 50 billion, which includes lactobacillus acidophilus; you can easily find this in the refrigerated section of your local health food or vitamin store. Also, avoid antibiotic use as this totally strips your intestines of the flora it needs to remain in balance. If you've ever had terrible stomach trouble, pain or diarrhea while using antibiotics, that's what is happening.

Enzymes are needed to survive because they are responsible for basically every chemical reaction in your body. Without enzymes, your body can't digest food properly. Unhealthy, toxic, and high free radical foods zap our enzyme supply, causing us major issues when it comes to breaking down foods properly. Enzyme levels also drop more and more quickly every decade as we age; this reduces our ability to properly absorb nutrients from food, causing all kinds of digestive issues and shortening life span. Supplement with bananas, mangoes, papayas, avocados, and sprouts, which are excellent enzyme-rich foods. Though when the food ripens, the enzymes start to deplete, so you must eat it within its peak time, pre-breakdown. Fortunately, there are also many Non-GMO, plant-based tablets and bottle suppliers that can help aid us with enzymes at our local health food vitamin shops. Take as directed by your doctor.

Dr. Kousouli's Secret Fit Tip #8
CHEW YOUR FOOD WELL BEFORE SWALLOWING

The other end of the "tube" that connects to your anus is your mouth. This may seem totally unrelated to the gut flora and bacteria that thrive in our bellies, but the truth is that how fast and how much we eat in a day actually affects our bodies' ability to break down and work through food. There are so many benefits to chewing thoroughly and slowly.

For one, you give your brain more time to catch up and release more of the peptide hormone that triggers the "full" sensation. For two, you're not going to choke. For three, your stomach will not feel bloated or stretched after just a few bites. And finally – the gut bacteria can actually work its way through the food instead of being smothered underneath a huge, impassable pile of junk.

Studies published in the *Journal of the Academy of Nutrition and Dietetics* in 2014 also explained that chewing our food slowly and well makes us less likely to swallow food-borne bacteria. When we chew through our food, we're breaking up the bacteria and neutralizing it. If those particles get into our stomach and wreak havoc on our gut bacteria, we get food poisoning, diarrhea, stomach pain, bloating, gas, etc.

I would prefer to enjoy the food I eat, taste it, savor it, and let my body gain nourishment from it. What about you?

Chapter Five:
Food Is Like Friends – Pick the Right Ones

"Every living cell in your body is made from the food you eat. If you consistently eat junk food then you'll have a junk body."
~ Jeanette Jenkins

Of course, everyone knows just how important it is to eat the right foods when you're trying to lose weight. What most people *don't know* is why certain foods are better, worse, or different than the others. In order to truly harness your body's full potential, you need to eat the right food and stop eating the wrong ones. This chapter will focus on the best and worst foods, and hopefully you'll have the ingredients you need for weight loss and healthy living.

Dr. Kousouli's Secret Fit Tip #9
CUT OUT REFINED WHEAT AND SUGAR

For the majority of my clients, this is the hardest part of any lifestyle change. Who doesn't love pasta, bread, and sugar?! Humans are actually wired to enjoy sugar and high-carb foods because, in our hunter-gatherer days, that meant more energy and more satiation after a meal. We ate our fill because we never knew when it was going to come around again.

Maybe our brains haven't advanced from our "Caveman Days," but we can train our brains to make better choices. Studies have proven that removing white, processed, overly refined sugar and wheat from our diets results in a withdrawal-like phenomenon. You're going to be tired, cranky, hungry; maybe even have headaches, fever, sore throat, joint pain, etc. But if something was good for you, do you think it would make your body feel like that when you didn't get it? No.

As gluten intolerance and Celiac disease is becoming more of a concern, more and more studies have been performed on the topic of refined wheat. Many, many studies are finding that refining wheat and grain down to flour actually triggers the same response that sugar has in the body. Our bodies go on high alert because there is nothing but empty calories, which causes your body and cells to literally 'freak out.'

Not only do these empty calories make us hungrier, they change our blood sugar, our gut health, and our overall health. Being in a state of constant inflammation from consuming foods like this leads to acidosis and dis-ease. Do yourself and your body a favor, and cut these foods out first. Ask your holistic health care provider for a food allergy test, which will also help you find the best foods that do not cause your body harm. Different blood types do well on certain foods, while on others they may be causing unnecessary internal inflammation.

Dr. Kousouli's Secret Fit Tip #10
DROP MEAT, GO PLANT BASED

We are guilty of assuming that meat has more protein than "rabbit food," and many try to shut down a plant-based diet because humans "are made to eat meat." While our ancestors most certainly needed to eat meat to survive, we actually have thousands more options that are more nutritious, more power-packed, and less harmful to our planet (and animals) than eating meat alone.

There are a number of *huge* benefits to enjoying a plant-based diet, varying from decreased food costs (meat costs keep increasing!) to increased longevity and happiness. Study upon study has found that plants actually provide just as much (if not more) protein than meats do, without the nasty side effect of influencing gut health or triggering an immune response. Prepared meats we digest also carry tons of antibiotics and hormones that go right into us; not to mention the tissue's infused energy from the anguish the animal felt as it was slaughtered!

In a U.S. News Health article written in January 2016, researchers discussed how red meat (and lots of it) is more connected with heart disease and diabetes in Americans. Moreover, meat doesn't contain enough of the fiber or other nutrients that people need to have a well-balanced diet.

Since the 1950's, meat and carbohydrates have taken over more than 50% of a traditional meal, compared to about 70% plant-based foods in the generations prior. Not surprisingly, since the 1950's, our overall health has decreased in dramatic ways (cancer, heart disease, obesity, etc.).

Carnivorous diets (mostly red meat intake) is known to increase our intake of cholesterol, saturated fat, and more hormones and antibiotics than our body can process. As you'll recall from the last chapter on gut health, antibiotics strip our body of the flora we need to protect our health.

Going plant-based doesn't necessarily mean *no meat ever*. It means eating "white meats," like chicken and turkey, and focusing on eating Omega-3 fatty fish like salmon. Try to replace your dinner meals with plant-based proteins and fish instead of red meat; your waistline and health will thank you for it!

Dr. Kousouli's Secret Fit Tip #11
USE PLANT PROTEIN POWDER TO FILL UP
HEALTHY & FAST

Now that you know the importance of plant-based food, you should extend this into your post-workout protein shakes and any supplements you want to take. A lot of people love using protein shakes as meal replacements too, which can help you lose weight quickly. But to make the most of these protein shakes, make sure it's plant-based, and doesn't have the artificial junk many mass retailers carry. Just put the powder in with a little bit of water, mix in some greens or chlorophyll powder, and go!

Dr. Kousouli's Secret Fit Tip #12
DRINK CHIA SEEDS TO FEEL FULL

Are you struggling with never feeling full? One trick I love to recommend is drinking chia seeds. A lot of people blend them into shakes, or even mix them with water. The seeds expand in liquid, and are packed with Omega 3 fatty acids. For a lot less than eating a big meal, you can have a quick snack and feel full for a long time afterwards.

Bonus: chia seeds have *tons* of fiber (good for gut health), protein (good for a plant-based diet), and generate more energy than most pre or post workout concoctions. There are tons of other ways to incorporate chia seeds into your diet, from chia seeds in whole grain foods to baking and more. Try them out and introduce them wherever you can!

Dr. Kousouli's Secret Fit Tip #13
DRINK APPLE CIDER VINEGAR + RAW MANUKA
HONEY & CINNAMON

A favorite drink of mine that I recommend to my patients is a mix of apple cider vinegar, raw Manuka honey, and cinnamon. You're probably thinking, "That sounds gross!" but it's really delicious, *and* it packs a powerful punch of antioxidants, nutrients, and more. Manuka honey has amazing anti-inflammatory properties, as does apple cider vinegar. Manuka honey and apple cider vinegar are also known to help with digestion, so if you struggle with gas, stomach pain, bloating, acid reflux, etc., this drink will do wonders!

The cinnamon is an anti-bacterial and adds a little sweetness and a little heat, and has long been known to help with the immune system, appetite, and even helping control blood sugar levels. Buy a high quality cinnamon powder, not just the generic stuff in a plastic bottle. Also make sure you get *raw* Manuka honey and *raw, unpasteurized* apple cider vinegar. Anything else has been processed and doesn't pack the full benefits.

Dr. Kousouli's Secret Fit Tip #14
USE DRIED FRUIT AS YOUR NEW GO-TO SNACK

I recommend keeping a dried fruit stash all around the house and in your drawers at work. Even hide some packaged raw, air-tight dry fruit (no artificial flavors and sugar added) where you can get at it quickly to munch on when you're feeling "hangry" (hungry + angry = poor food choices). This is also helpful to people who are trying to kick a sugar addiction, are hypoglycemic, or are on the go a lot.

You can make good decisions when you arm yourself with a healthy, sweet snack that curbs cravings and gives you just enough energy to keep you going. There are some DELICIOUS dried fruits out there, have you tried them? Check your local farmer's market fruit aisle.

Dr. Kousouli's Secret Fit Tip #15
WATCH WHAT YOU DRINK

We usually overlook what we drink, as long as it's not the obviously bad sugary sodas. But there are dangers with drinking too much coffee, energy and workout drinks, sweetened and artificial juices, and even milk! If you're watching what you're eating, you need to watch what you drink, too.

To my clients, I usually recommend replacing coffee with tea, especially oolong and green tea as they boost metabolism and are amazing for immunity. I also address the hidden sugars in their favorite energy or coffee drinks. Most "fruit juice" contains 23g of sugar in 8oz, while our daily recommended intake is 25-35g, according to the Food and Drug Administration. Drinking natural, sugar-free, or cold-pressed fruit juices will help you cut this down drastically.

You may be thinking, "It says sugar-free!" if you're a diet soda fan, but those substitute real sugar with insane levels of dangerous chemicals, like aspartame which has been connected to an increased risk of brain cancer! In addition, your body can't process the ingredients, and instead your body is going to transfer the "sugar imposters" into fat. Cut out the diet soda, and cut down your waistline! Go for half a packet of the powdered coconut flakes for adding a 'touch' of healthy sweetness.

Then we have cow's milk, which many of us consider to be part of a healthy daily dose of Vitamin D. Well, it's also an unhealthy amount of antibiotics and hormones from the cows which, studies show, are connected to increased antibiotic resistance, cancer, allergies, and bad bacteria present in humans who drink it. According to an article published in 2015 by Global Healing Center, cows milk also contains pus, blood, and more "yummy" stuff. Some researchers believe this is why so many people have digestive issues so young, because of the excessive amount of cow's milk most Americans consume. Cut out the cow's milk, and try coconut, hemp, or almond milk instead. They're delicious, and they don't have a cocktail of terrible things inside.

Dr. Kousouli's Secret Fit Tip #16
DROP THE SALT

Salt is known to be bad for your overall health, and you probably know that people cut out salt after a heart attack. But why cut it out if you want to lose weight? Salty food is, after all, delicious. Basically it boils down to this: salt affects the function of every organ in our body, bloats our cells, and prevents proper filtering and processing in our body. More and more studies are finding that high sodium diets (the entire American diet) lead to hypertension, vitamin deficiency, and even cognitive impairments, according to professors in nutrition interviewed for a LiveScience article in 2012.

For weight loss, cutting down salt means your body will be able to shed the bloated water weight it has accrued. Salt holds not only water but other vitamins, so cutting out salt and sodium-laden foods will let your body filter properly once again. Aside from losing weight, you could be saving your life. Extended sodium intake at American diet levels leads to congestive heart failure, kidney and liver failure, and is connected to diabetes and autoimmune diseases as well.

Dr. Kousouli's Secret Fit Tip #17
HOT PEPPERS AND SPICES HELP TURN UP METABOLISM

Spicy foods are great for adding flavor to food, especially when you're learning how to incorporate healthier choices and are craving the more savory/sugary/salty foods. I always recommend adding garlic to food – the freshly chopped stuff, not the powder – for flavor and a little heat. Garlic is an anti-inflammatory, great for your immune system, and is high in vitamins. It's also known to decrease risk of heart disease and high cholesterol, and speeds up metabolism while detoxifying your body of heavy metals, according to Authority Nutrition.

I also recommend capsaicin, which is found in chili peppers and jalapeños. Capsaicin is thought to speed up metabolism because of the increased "heat energy," which helps burn more fat. In a study done by the University of Wyoming in 2012, it was found that mice who consumed small percentages of capsaicin even with a high-fat diet lost fat. Capsaicin also increases overall health and immune function, and is even being studied in connection to cancer reduction, according to a CBS News interview that aired in February 2015. Add some garlic and some peppers to your weekly diet, and enjoy flavor and health!

Dr. Kousouli's Secret Fit Tip #18
ADD PSYLLIUM HUSKS TO YOUR DAILY DIET

We've already gone over the merits of adding fiber to your daily diet and paying attention to your bathroom routine for gut health in Secret Fit Tip #6. According to most sources, you need about 25 to 30 grams of fiber a day to keep your stomach and bowels happy, but most Americans only get about 15g and that's from supplements, "fortified" (aka processed) foods, and so on. I recommend adding psyllium husk fiber to your daily diet because it takes care of your daily intake in one fell swoop, without wondering if you've had enough food to account for your fiber intake (remember: we don't want to have to count all day long!).

Psyllium husk fiber is made from plant seeds, and when ground down it becomes a water-soluble fiber that keeps our bodies and bowels in great regulation. Adding 10g of psyllium husk to your daily diet will help keep your bowel movements regular, and will help you make sure your intestines are cleared out. Studies are also showing that psyllium husk fiber and other plant-based water-soluble fibers like it can help with indigestion and diseases like Crohn's disease. Add it to your daily regimen and see the benefits yourself.

Chapter Six:
Addressing it All; Spirit, Body, and Mind

"Mirrors are perpetually deceitful. They lie and steal your true self.
They reveal only what your mind believes it sees."

~ Dee Remy

The Kousouli® Method 4R Intervention System of Healing

M y experience with the different aspects of chiropractic care, clinical research, energy healing, clairvoyant meditation, hypnosis, and personal experiences in and out of the clinic, both as a doctor and as a patient, have helped me develop the 4R Kousouli® Method of Health. **The main goal of the Kousouli® Method is to address vital energy loss in 4 main arenas (spiritual, mental, emotional, and physical) by utilizing the nervous system.**

The Kousouli® Method 4R Intervention System gives patients a daily checklist and simple structure for making sure they are on point to "Rejuvenate the Body, Empower the Mind, and Free the Soul." When the body is overweight, fatigued, or depressed, it is not in its normal homeostatic flow, which is where the Kousouli® Method steps in.

The following pages include diagrams of three main circles, two of which are cycle states of health. The first cycle reflects where most people are when they feel something is wrong or feel ill. Because of accumulated poor lifestyle habits and neglect over time, they feel lousy and seek out a healthcare provider to deal with the physical body. The first cycle (left) reflects the negative aspects of health. The center circle represents the **Kousouli® Method 4R Intervention Health System.** When one becomes proactive by utilizing the

Kousouli® Method, they complete the 4 steps of ***Remove, Revive, Rebuild, and Reset.*** This is where change starts, and if maintained during a set care plan over time, favorable results will start to appear. The third circle (right) reflects the positive benefits of health after incorporating the Kousouli® Method. If maintained, the patient stays in this positive cycle unless neglect pulls the process back to the negative cycle.

KOUSOULI METHOD

RESULTS

GOAL
Stay on the program for positive results to manifest. It takes time to reverse years of negative toxic living.

CELL, TISSUE, ORGAN, SYSTEM, AND BODY HEALTH

OPTIMAL POTENTIAL

PAIN FREE

HEALING

HOMEOSTASIS

INCREASED ENERGY

ALKALINE PH

+ CYCLE

Connection
Regular chiropractic care keeps your nervous system operating interference-free, allowing your body to handle its daily demands stress-free.

Flow
Hydrated, Nourished, Oxygenated, Clean Air, Flexibility, Proper Elimination, Active Lifestyle

Ease
Peaceful Harmony, Mental Clarity, Homeostasis, (+) Emotional Stability, Feelings of Love, Abundance, Gratitude

Purity
Low/No load: Electrical pollution (cell phone, T.V, computer use), radiation, drugs, alcohol, smoking, parasites, metal poisoning, allergens, oxides, junk food

---

INCREASE MOTION

PROMOTE HEALING

IMPROVE CSF/BP & LYMPH FLOW

REDUCE STRESS FACTORS

REGENERATE TISSUE

IMPROVE MOTION

INCREASE SELF WORTH

REDUCE ACIDS

KOUSOULI METHOD

2. REVIVE
Chiropractic adjustments reduce spinal stress and open communication pathways from the brain to every cell, tissue, and organ in the body.

3. REBUILD
Hydrate. Nourish. Oxygenate. Supplementation. Exercise, Stretch. Deep Tissue Re-organization.

1. REMOVE
Drugs, Alcohol, Caffeine. Parasites. Metal Toxicity. Allergens. Electro-Magnetic Radiation. Scar Tissue. Junk Food. Environmental & Occupational Hazards.

4. RESET
Prayer. Meditation. Visualization. Hypnotic Suggestion. Emotional Reconditioning.

Those with healthy lives make daily healthy choices. Adding the steps of *Remove, Revive, Rebuild, and Reset* into your life over time will help you regain health.

PROACTIVE

START
When seeking lost health, you should first look at your lifestyle choices and identify what is causing toxic buildup. Then a decision to be *proactive* about changing your negative lifestyle choices must be met with a method that works.

NEGLECT

To remain in the positive cycle without losing any progress by relapse, you must decide your health is a priority worth maintaining over the course of your life, not just once in a while. Neglecting to do steps 1 through 4 will bring you back to a negative quality of life.

CELL, TISSUE, ORGAN, SYSTEM, AND BODY DEATH

LOW POTENTIAL

SUFFERING

PAIN

SORES

FATIGUE

OVERWEIGHT

ACIDIC PH

— CYCLE

Stagnation
Dehydrated, Malnourished, De-Oxygenated, Poor Air, Stiffness, Poor Elimination, Sedentary Lifestyle

Dis-Connection
Without chiropractic care, physical, chemical & emotional stresses overload the body causing spinal interference. Over time, this leads to pain and poor function.

Dis-Ease
Lack of Harmony, Mental Clarity Homeostasis, (-) Emotional Overload, Worst, Relationships, Feelings of Fear, Hate, Resentment, Anxiety

Toxicity
High load: Electrical pollution (cell phone, T.V, computer use), radiation, drugs, alcohol, smoking, parasites, metal poisoning, allergens, oxides, junk food

The success of the method is due to the focus on the 4R *continuous processes*:

1. ***Remove the* toxins.** Cautiously limit or remove (as much as possible) all avoidable drug use (prescription, over-the-counter, or recreational), alcohol consumption, caffeine, sodas, smoking, intestinal worms & parasites, heavy metal toxicity, allergens, electro-magnetic radiation, old scar tissue build-up, junk food and fast food, environmental and occupational ergonomic hazards.

2. ***Revive* the nervous system utilizing correct chiropractic care.** Chiropractic adjustments reduce spinal stress and open vital communication pathways from the brain to every cell, tissue, and organ in the body.

3. ***Rebuild* the body through whole food nutrition and exercise.** Proper hydration, nourishment, oxygenation, supplementation, exercise, stretching, and deep tissue re-organization of spinal muscle attachments.

4. ***Reset* your thoughts and programming.** Prayer, meditation, visualization, hypnotic suggestion, Kousouli Neural Emotive Reconditioning (KNER®), and proper mind and body rest will ensure that the whole process is perpetuated within yourself, and you continue to reap the benefits for the rest of your life.

Going through the Kousouli® Method 4R intervention system will ensure you get the 5th 'R' too; ***Recovery!*** My simple message is: Those who are "Hollywood skinny" are not just thin. They possess strength, unlimited energy, and youthful and healthy lives as a result of making healthy choices. Don't lie to yourself thinking that just going to the gym, eating a few days' worth of salads instead of meat, one day of yoga, or a week of Hollywood's latest detox craze will get you healthy. To stay in the positive cycle, without losing any progress by relapse, you *must* decide your health is a priority worth maintaining over the course of your life - not just for a week or a few months.

Staying in the Positive Cycle

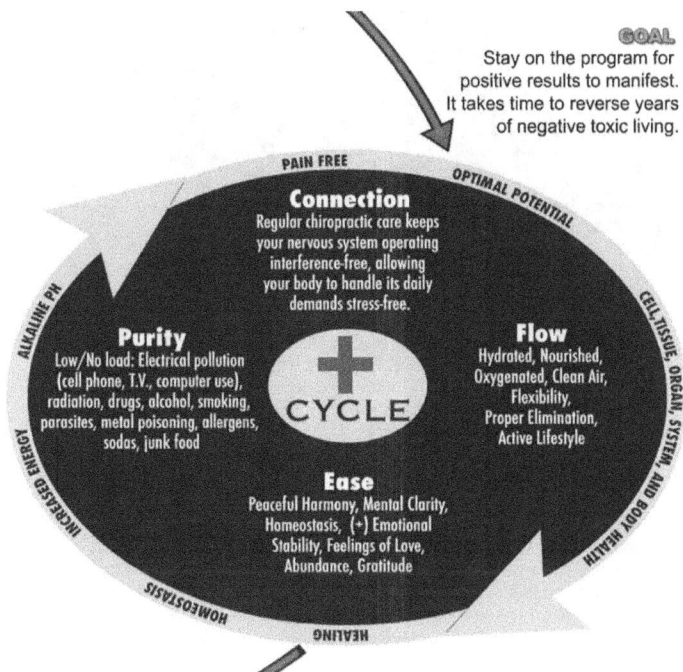

GOAL
Stay on the program for positive results to manifest. It takes time to reverse years of negative toxic living.

PAIN FREE

OPTIMAL POTENTIAL

Connection
Regular chiropractic care keeps your nervous system operating interference-free, allowing your body to handle its daily demands stress-free.

ALKALINE PH

Purity
Low/No load: Electrical pollution (cell phone, T.V., computer use), radiation, drugs, alcohol, smoking, parasites, metal poisoning, allergens, sodas, junk food

CYCLE

CELL, TISSUE, ORGAN, SYSTEM, AND BODY HEALTH

Flow
Hydrated, Nourished, Oxygenated, Clean Air, Flexibility, Proper Elimination, Active Lifestyle

INCREASED ENERGY

Ease
Peaceful Harmony, Mental Clarity, Homeostasis, (+) Emotional Stability, Feelings of Love, Abundance, Gratitude

HEALTH

HOMEOSTASIS

HEALING

Connection: Regular chiropractic care keeps your nervous system operating in an interference-free fashion, allowing your body to handle its daily demands in a stress-free manner.

Flow: Incorporating proper hydration, nourishment, oxygen, clean air, flexibility, proper elimination, and an active lifestyle will ensure a smooth flow of energy within your body.

Ease: Having peaceful purpose, harmony, mental clarity, homeostasis, positive emotional stability, feelings of love, abundance, and gratitude for yourself and others will keep you in a positive frame of mind.

Purity: Avoid or remove electrical pollution (cellular phone, televisions, and computers), radiation, drugs, alcohol, smoking, parasites, metal poisoning, allergens, sodas, caffeine overload, junk, or fast food.

Reverting Back to the Negative Cycle through Neglect

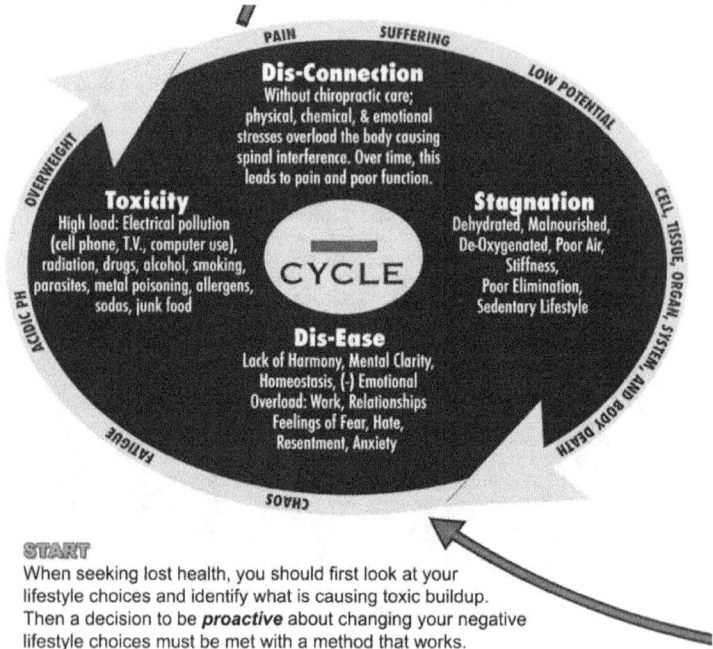

When seeking lost health, you should first look at your lifestyle choices and identify what is causing toxic buildup. Then a decision to be **proactive** about changing your negative lifestyle choices must be met with a method that works.

Dis-connection: Irregular, discontinuous, or complete lack of chiropractic care; physical, chemical, and emotional stresses all compound spinal overload. Over time, this miscommunication of brain-to-body leads to pain and poor function.

Stagnation: Staying in a dehydrated condition, receiving improper nutrition, no or low supplementation, poor air or water quality, lymph flow backup, poor elimination, and a sedentary lifestyle are cardinal signs for bringing your health down.

Dis-Ease: Lack of harmony, mental clarity, negative emotional stresses, work or relationship stress overload, feelings of fear, hate, resentment and anxiety all will contribute to disease conditions.

Toxicity: High load of electro-magnetic pollution, radiation, drugs, alcohol, smoking, parasites, heavy metal poisoning, allergens, sodas, and junk food will result in an overall imbalance and a downslide of your health condition.

It becomes apparent from the above points that most of your health is a matter of lifestyle choice; being able to regulate your temptations and not resorting to the lazier lower vibration path at every whim. Sometimes, taking the tougher route ultimately proves to be wiser, healthier, and perhaps easier in the long run. Consistency is key in maintaining a healthy condition, and the more consistent you are with your good habits and lifestyle choices the better you will be served by your body.

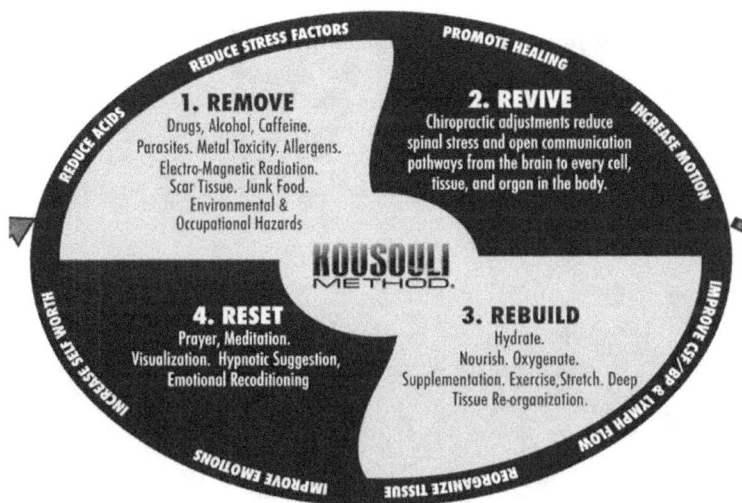

REDUCE STRESS FACTORS   PROMOTE HEALING

REDUCE ACIDS   INCREASE MOTION

1. REMOVE
Drugs, Alcohol, Caffeine.
Parasites. Metal Toxicity. Allergens.
Electro-Magnetic Radiation.
Scar Tissue. Junk Food.
Environmental &
Occupational Hazards

2. REVIVE
Chiropractic adjustments reduce
spinal stress and open communication
pathways from the brain to every cell,
tissue, and organ in the body.

KOUSOULI
METHOD.

4. RESET
Prayer, Meditation.
Visualization. Hypnotic Suggestion,
Emotional Recoditioning

3. REBUILD
Hydrate.
Nourish. Oxygenate.
Supplementation. Exercise, Stretch. Deep
Tissue Re-organization.

INCREASE SELF WORTH   IMPROVE CSF & LYMPH FLOW

IMPROVE EMOTIONS   REORGANIZE TISSUE

Those with healthy lives make daily healthy
choices. Adding the steps of *Remove,*
Revive, Rebuild, and Reset into
your life *over time* will help you *regain health.*

The Kousouli® Method 4R Intervention Health System is continuously being adapted through clinical application and research. When correctly applied, it has shown successful symptom reduction or elimination of headaches, dizziness, fatigue/low energy, carpel tunnel, whiplash pains, muscle spasms, joint pains, neck pain, back pain, allergies, depression, hormonal imbalances, fibromyalgia, numbness, limb tingling, IBS, asthma, acid reflux/GERD, arthritis, insomnia, and toxicity - just to name a few. The Kousouli® Method through KNER® also takes into account the spiritual, mental, and emotional aspects of health, which usually manifest into the physical plane as pain and dis-ease. By accessing specific energy points and balancing these points from leaking, the individual can focus their energy on healing with quicker results.

This system's powerful technique of replenishing health naturally goes beyond the surface scope of this book and is taught privately to interested practitioners at live seminar events.

Details can be found at www.KousouliMethod.com.

Chapter Seven:
Detoxification

"You are what you eat."

~ Victor Lindlahr

As I note in my book, *BE A MASTER® OF MAXIMUM HEAL-ING*, any health issue that brings the body out of homeostasis must be looked at as a whole body issue - not just as a singular issue. Obesity, acidity, toxic overload, fatigue, depression, etc. all are effects of a deeper-seated issue. My method, the Kousouli® Method, looks at many aspects of ill health and can help you get to the root of the problem.

Once your body is detoxified properly, it's like a clean slate. Everything that you put into your body has the ability to support (or upset) your health and weight goals.

Dr. Kousouli's Secret Fit Tip #19
ONE WEEK FAST EACH SEASON

If you've never done a fast before, you're probably thinking, "That sounds miserable!" A lot of the fasting programs on the market today *are* miserable and - worse yet - ineffective. My recommendation, rather than these crazy concoctions and one day flushes, is to do a cold pressed juice fast for a week each season.

This means no solid food for a week, which allows your body to "clean the pipes" so to speak, and loosen up anything that has remained within the folds of your digestive system. There are many local stores now that offer a week's worth of healthy juices that will help clean you out and sustain your vital force.

Why juice? After the first day of fasting, your body starts looking at its own energy (and fat) stores to help convert into energy so that it can keep functioning. This means that glycogen, what your body uses for energy to rebuild and work, is going to get burned. Fruit juice has enough sugar to restore the glycogen in your body, giving your body the energy it needs. This means it will zone in on that leftover fat, and burn through it faster than your energy reserves.

You won't go hungry, and you will give your gut a very much-needed reboot. Doing it four times a year helps keep your body clean and efficient. I recommend "keeping with the seasons," as this helps you get more in tune with the natural cycles of food and your body. During each new season, our bodies go through changes just like the earth does.

Removal of the "Acid State"

Fasting is just one component of the *Remove phase* in **the Kousouli®️ Method.** The *Remove* component is so important because, if you are struggling with weight or health, odds are you have entered an "acid state."

Our bodies work under a finely regulated homeostatic balance of acids and bases (a.k.a. alkalis) 24/7, 365 days a year. The body also produces its own neutralizing buffers to keep the overall acidity under control. By encouraging a proper whole food diet and removing toxic loads through the *Remove* phase of care, the body is given a chance to come back to balance and work better in the *Rebuild* phase.

But if we have acidity naturally occurring in our bodies, why is an over-accumulation of acids bad? Acidosis can affect the colon, making it hard to flush out fecal matter. Any leftovers can actually enter the bloodstream, which leads to toxicity. The heart relies on alkaline (less acidic) pH levels. If the body is operating at a higher acidity, the heart rate increases, and the heart cannot properly oxygenate. Acidity in the stomach can cause just about any bad stomach issue you can think of, and is probably the most obvious display of acidity in our bodies.

Other areas affected by acidosis include the liver (which works only in an alkaline environment), the kidneys (that filter out acidic products), the small intestine, the pancreas, and the entire lymphatic system.

Dr. Kousouli's Secret Fit Tip #20
DETOX THE BLOOD AND DIGESTIVE TRACT

Detoxification is defined as the process that helps you get rid of toxins, by either neutralizing them or transforming them into benign forms. Detoxification also incorporates removal of congestions and excess mucus. The first part of any effective corrective program is toxin removal through digestive tract cleansing which ultimately become the contents in the circulatory system. These two are intimately entwined and both must be addressed if one is serious about weight loss.

Benefiting From a Good Colon Cleansing Program

Proper colon detoxification programs prepare your body for optimal health by eradicating mucoid plaque. Colon hydrotherapy, psyllium, home enemas, and herbal colon cleansers that incorporate a combination of internal cleansing herbs are all part of an ideal detoxification program. Someone on a typical Western diet accumulates 8 meals of undigested food and waste within their colon at any given time. Someone living on a high fiber diet may accumulate only 2 or 3 meals between our bodies' natural expulsions of waste. Appropriate intestinal cleansing will help shed accumulated food debris (and pounds)!

Detox with Caution

A strict and intelligent detox, diet, and regular exercise program is required to burn fat cells and keep obesity in check. A congested liver, gallbladder, and large intestine are almost always compromised in obesity. See a holistic nutritionist and doctor of functional medicine for toxic heavy metal removal (your health issue may be connected to a thyroid condition). Have your doctor check for leaky gut syndrome, candida albicans (yeast syndrome) overgrowth, and celiac disease (gluten intolerance). Do a liver, gallbladder, colon, and parasite cleanse (which may lead to weight loss), and combine this with regular chiropractic care to open your life force (chi) and lessen stress on your spine and joints.

Stop all greasy, fatty, and fried junk foods, as well as alcohol, smoking, wheat, dairy, refined sugar, and artificial flavor intake immediately! Removing these foods counts as part of your detox process, so don't neglect it and think, "Well, my detox will take care of that!"

Hydrate well, use digestive enzymes, drink raw apple cider vinegar, eat dark green vegetables, drink liquid chlorophyll, eat dulse flakes, mung beans, mushrooms, adzuki beans, broccoli, kale, cauliflower, spirulina, tofu, ginger, laminaria (kelp), sargassum seaweed, truffles, use psyllium, flaxseed, red pepper (capsaicin), triphala, and cinnamon in your diet. Eat for energy; do not eat emotionally, which leads to feeling guilty or shameful.

What to Expect From a Detox

When performing a system detox, it's usually recommended that you start slowly. The body will go through withdrawal symptoms, especially if the patient is addicted to high glycemic carbohydrates, diet and caffeine drinks, smoking, or drinking. A successful program leads to release of accumulated food colors like RED #40, or additives like MSG, parasites, yeast (candida), and harmful bacteria overgrowth. This waste leaves the tissues and enters your blood system as it travels for neutralization and elimination. This is why patients will usually experience issues like: fever, nausea, headaches, chills, ulcers, skin rashes, thirst, increased urination, loss of appetite, eye pain, difficulty sleeping, extreme drowsiness and fatigue, diarrhea, muscle soreness, lack of motivation, etc.

This detox side effect phenomenon is termed a "healing crisis" and generally lasts for a 1 to 2 week period after starting a detox. Although it may not seem like it at first, this is a good thing, as it means the body has begun cleaning up toxins and is beginning to repair and heal. Healing only occurs after the toxins have been dealt with and the body can start to rebuild in a healthier state.

After a proper cleansing period, and after you've started taking care of your gut, spine, and mental health, you will notice your body changing for the better. The key is to stay on the program and give it time to work for you, as your body reprograms itself from the inside out.

Cleansing by Chelation Therapy

Chelation is the process by which a metal or mineral links to another substance, which is how aspirin, antibiotics, vitamins, minerals and trace elements all work in our body. Intravenous chelation therapy is a non-invasive, safe, and effective methodology that reverses and slows the progression of atherosclerosis and other age-related and degenerative diseases. This therapy utilizes a small amino acid called ethylene diamine tetra acetic acid (commonly abbreviated EDTA), which links with harmful loose metals in the body and excretes them out.

This is highly beneficial for people who have a number of health issues exacerbated by their weight, or who have developed increased cholesterol or other levels due to their food intake. On average, 85 percent of chelation patients that have the procedure improve significantly.

It has been observed to be beneficial for heart attacks, leg pain, blocked arteries, stroke, diabetes, gangrene, and also cancer. It has also been considered as an alternative to bypass surgery, or angioplasty and stents. Rather than having invasive options for circulatory disorders such as coronary artery disease, or cerebral vascular disease, EDTA chelation therapy has been considered a better option in combination with a well-balanced diet and healthy lifestyle.

This outpatient procedure is mostly a painless treatment, with minimal discomfort and a normal lifestyle while doing infusion. With current advanced methods there is also the oral tablet, and now also an option of suppository chelation tabs which can be inserted nightly through the anal passage and excreted easily in the morning. Both of the administration methods are risk-free and non-toxic, when compared with other available drug treatment options. This method also has scored highly in terms of eliminating death rates generally caused by other conventional invasive therapy.

Find a chelation therapy clinic in your area, and do your own research. You are your best advocate, so consider your findings before jumping into action.

Chapter Eight:
It's Not About The Numbers!

"The definition of insanity is doing the same thing over and over again, expecting different results."

~ Albert Einstein

How many times have you tried to lose weight by downloading the latest calorie counter app, checking the packages on all your favorite foods, and stripping down naked when you use a scale just to lose a few extra ounces? We are told by the media and by the "skinny people police" that counting calories and watching your weight is where the real results are at. But if that was true, all of the people that feed the $300 billion diet industry would be, well, "Hollywood skinny." It's clearly not working, so maybe it's time to change the way we approach weight loss and "dieting."

Dr. Kousouli's Secret Fit Tip #21
STOP COUNTING

One of the worst myths about weight loss is that you have to count the calories that each food contains. Calories are, by definition, the measure of energy. Why would you want to worry about how much energy you're putting into your body if you're using it and consuming it positively?

Change your approach, and take what you're putting into your body as a whole, rather than just thinking about the calories. I have heard from numerous clients that this changes their approach to weight loss and food in general, and that it helps them lose weight faster and *keep it off*.

Instead of worrying about numbers and going crazy keeping track, focus on food *quality*. Think of your body as a Ferrari that needs premium gas to run smooth. You wouldn't feed your Ferrari low grade gas, so why would you feed your body low grade food? The greener, cleaner, and less fried/oily/processed the food is; the better. Another great trick to help your mind deal with food quantity is to throw out all your big plates and eat off of smaller plates. When you put food on it, it will look like a much larger portion and you will be more ready to be full quicker.

After that, talk with a functional medicine doctor, and have them help you remove all nonprescription and prescription drugs if possible, and look into the benefits of removing chlorine and fluoride from your water.

Dr. Kousouli's Secret Fit Tip #22
HIDE THE SCALE

Yes, you can drive yourself crazy counting pounds or kilograms. Just standing on the scale triggers a stress response in most people, and to put yourself through that daily or weekly isn't healthy. "How much do I weigh this time?" or "Oh god, I shouldn't have eaten that because now the scale will show I'm heavier!" runs through our heads, when we should really be thinking about how much progress we've made, how much better we feel when we're eating healthy food, etc. Thinking more about how heavy you are rather than how much lighter you are also tells yourself you've already been defeated before you've begun. No one wants to lose anything- we want to WIN! Use the scale when you know you have exchanged enough fat for energy and vitality. Change your interaction with the scale, and bring it out only after a considerable amount of time detoxing and weight training to see how much you've actually WON!

Dr. Kousouli's Secret Fit Tip #23
UNDERSTAND RESTING METABOLISM

If you're familiar with the hit show *The Biggest Loser* where people compete to lose the most weight, you're probably also familiar with the contestants' struggles to keep off their weight after the show's end. For a while, people just assumed that it was because the ex-contestants weren't sticking to a strict diet or exercising like crazy. But then more and more contestants were struggling, and started packing on the pounds, even while keeping up with their trainers' expectations.

Gina Kolata wrote a fantastic article in the *New York Times* in April, 2016 documenting this phenomenon. Researchers finally got involved after the 13th contestant reported excess weight gain, and what they found is this: exercise and dieting decreases your resting metabolism. This means that your body will burn through food and calories slower than it did before because it's expecting to need them.

Once you establish a workout routine, a specific daily diet of foods, and change your approach entirely, you have to understand and work to your body's new reality. In order to keep the weight off, you're going to have to slowly adapt to the changes. This is why fad diets and excessive exercise only to hit a goal weight **do not work!** Science has proven it.

Chapter Nine:
Tips to Trick Your Brain Into Making Healthy Choices

"There are lots of people in this world who spend so much time watching their health that they haven't the time to enjoy it."
~ Josh Billings

Dr. Kousouli's Secret Fit Tip #24
DON'T ADD EXTRAS TO THE MEAL; GO LIGHT

You could eat all of the vegetables in the world, but if you're adding on bad carbohydrates and creamy fats on top of that, you might as well just forget the vegetables all together. I always recommend eating a light meal, even for dinner. When you're eating vegetables and healthy foods, your body is going to feel fuller faster, because you're getting nutrient-rich foods for your body to work on without burdening it with heavy digestion.

Tips: don't add a lot of butter, oil, or other high-fat toppings or seasonings. If you need a little fat for cooking, try coconut oil instead of butter. Less trans fat, more deliciousness! I also recommend leaving the pasta or carbohydrate sides out. I promise – you *will* feel full eating a plant-based diet so give your food a little space on the plate. If you're having a hard time cutting out the breads or pastas as your side, try vegetable alternatives like zucchini pasta or baking with cauliflower instead of wheat. There are so many options out there, grab a cookbook!

Dr. Kousouli's Secret Fit Tip #25
COOK AT HOME; EAT OUT LESS

Everyone loves eating out, so I understand that this is probably a hard step to follow. But when you cook at home, you're essentially signaling to your body (and the universe): "I am in control of my choices, I am going to make a healthy meal, and I'm going to enjoy it." You won't be tempted by the 8-cheese pasta dish that the restaurant down the street offers, and you're less likely to overdrink or overeat.

To make this step a little easier, why not have a dinner party with the people you usually go out to eat with? Invite them over, cook them an amazing meal, and share food and laughter. Having this support group will also help boost your mood and keep you busy in conversation. Nobody wants to feel like a shut-in; the more you learn to love cooking at home by controlling what you make and eat, the longer the weight will stay off. So make sure you're making every effort to *enjoy* this, rather than hating it!

Dr. Kousouli's Secret Fit Tip #26
REMOVE ALL DISTRACTIONS WHILE EATING

How often do you plop yourself down in front of the TV or your computer while you eat? How many times do you pick up fast food and just inhale whatever is in the bag while you drive to your next meeting? Have you ever stood over the sink, scarfing down yesterday's lunch just so you can run off to the next event? We're all so guilty of this one, and it's part of why we're so disconnected to food and our weight.

When we're eating without thinking about the food, or when we're rushing around while we eat, we're triggering a cortisol (stress) response in our bodies that our bodies begin to associate with food. What happens when cortisol flares up? All other hormones get tamped down, including the ones that make us feel full and relaxed. By eating quickly or not paying attention, we're essentially telling our bodies that feeding time is a stressful time – eat and run! Save what you can!

To break this cycle, we need to learn to actually acknowledge the food we eat and take time to digest. Turn off the car (if you really have to eat on the go), turn off the TV, sit down at a table, and eat. Talking to people is fine, but really focus on the act of eating. Bless the food with a grateful mindset, look at what you're eating by slowly chewing it, taste every bite, and enjoy it! Your body will have the time it needs to process what you're putting in, and your brain will enter a state of calm. You'll feel better, and you'll help yourself lose weight. Really!

Dr. Kousouli's Secret Fit Tip #27
SLEEP FOR BETTER HORMONE METABOLISM

Losing sleep is not good for anyone, despite what your friends who are pushing you to go to the club at midnight tell you. How many times have you compared the handful of hours you slept last night with coworkers, parents, or your friends or family? "I only got 3 hours of sleep, and I'm up and running already!" First all, we need to address this attitude, because sleep deprivation is *not* an admirable trait. Let's go for healthy instead of sleep-deprived, shall we?

Sleep is directly correlated to your health and waistline as well. You'd think that lying down and sleeping would make you *more* obese, but your body and brain do its best rebuilding and working at night when you're asleep. In a book called *Endocrine Development* published in 2010, researchers compiled years and years of evidence indicating that sleep deprivation results in: increases in cortisol (the stress hormone that makes many of us overeat) and increased ghrelin (the hormone that says "I'm hungry!"). So it's not shocking that this is correlated to a continuous cycle of increased stress, less sleep, and more eating and obesity.

The other important thing about sleep is that it helps us burn through our stores of glucose, which turn into fat stores if not properly used. When we're not sleeping, our body isn't using it, and we get larger and larger. So next time you're thinking, "I can pull an all-nighter, it's fine!" – think about how you want to lose weight, how much you've struggled, and call it a night. You'll thank yourself in the morning.

> **Dr. Kousouli's Secret Fit Tip #28**
> **BRUSH YOUR TEETH AFTER DINNER**

Are you one of those people who always finds yourself buried in the fridge 10 minutes before you go to bed? Do you lay in bed thinking of a midnight snack? While a lot of this is going to take sheer will power to break these habits, try this one little trick: brush your teeth earlier.

I've heard of people brushing their teeth after they're totally done with dinner because it helps them "cleanse their palate" and makes them feel like they don't want to eat. You're less likely to eat after you brush and floss your teeth; it's like not wanting to lie in your bed after you've made it. Work these quirks to your advantage, and tweak other routines to help you break bad habits!

> **Dr. Kousouli's Secret Fit Tip #29**
> **USE IMAGING PROGRAMS TO YOUR BENEFIT**

A common manifestation technique I use to help my patients visualize their thinner, future selves is to show them an edited photo of themselves. They usually gasp in excitement, as they can't believe that's their future, slimmed-down, healthier self staring back at them in the picture. They love using the image to "shoot for the goal." Want to try it out and put the photo on your vision board or tape it to your workout equipment? It's pretty simple! Just take your photo (a new one or recent full body shot you already have) and load it up on any imaging software like *Photoshop*. Use the liquefy tool to slim down your image to how you wish yourself to look. Or if you want a professional to do it, send your digital photo to a photo editor and ask them to edit a slimmed down version of you. There are many inexpensive and professional photo editors who will make the image of the 'future you' look very realistic.

Use this image as inspiration for your weight loss and when you get to the target weight, take a new photo next to the altered copy and celebrate how much better you look in person than the digital image!

Chapter Ten:
Exercise for Total Body Health

"Those who think they have not time for bodily exercise will sooner or later have to find time for illness."

~ Edward Stanley

Our days are often structured around work, driving, or generally moving around in ways that aren't great for our body. It's no wonder that we gain weight and keep it on when we don't ever move our body in the ways it needs to be moved. Who has time for an hour of yoga every day? Honestly, not many. We need a fast, easy way to properly extend our spinal column; this is where the *Kousouli® Spinal Stretches (KSS®)* come in very handy. You'll extend your spinal column and stretch body parts you didn't even know you had – in basically no time at all!

> ### Dr. Kousouli's Secret Fit Tip #30
> ### STRETCH DAILY

The *Kousouli® Spinal Stretches (KSS®)* provide a number of benefits for the body, mind, and spirit, which can translate into a happier, healthier, thinner you. **A few benefits include:**

- Spinae muscle groups become more erect. This improves your posture, making you look young and healthier.

- Stretches improve circulation, which improves health all around.

- Stretches release tension, which helps reduce stress and negative emotions that can lead to negative relationships with food.

- Stretches burn calories, which obviously helps us lose weight and look great.

- Stretches release endorphins, which improve your mood and the energy you exude.

- Stretches increase oxygen flow to brain and lungs, which makes you more alert and aware.

- Muscles will be strengthened and stamina will increase, which allows you to be more physical and active, furthering your overall health.

Some notes before you begin:

- Always consult your doctor before beginning any exercise or stretching program like KSS®.

- If you feel pain when performing any movements - stop immediately.

- Begin your KSS® gently - do not 'jump right in' forcefully. Give yourself time to adapt.

- If you have had a joint replacement or are just coming out of surgery, simply limit, restrict, or avoid major movements.

- KSS® movements and methods may be modified and adapted to suit an individual's age, needs, and abilities. Do the modified versions labeled 'M' if the original stretch is too difficult for you.

- A KSS® program for seniors or arthritis sufferers may be applied slowly, and modified gradually over a period of time, depending on skill level. Move your joints slowly through a full range of motion several times, to help enhance over-all circulation, and decrease any stiffness. KSS® may be re-sumed once tenderness has diminished and your doctor al-lows you back to total activity.

- Rest painful, inflamed, or hot joints with a cold ice compress at 15-30 minute intervals, and discontinue for the time be-ing if pain occurs.

- Always breathe deeply down into your diaphragm (not chest), and allow unrestricted flow of your airway while do-ing KSS® movements.

- Be sure to use a pillow or soft mat for any joints (like the knees) that make constant contact with the ground during modified stretching.

- Practice good technique; do not overextend joints beyond the normal range of motion. Maintain good form and pos-ture.

- Hydrate often throughout the day (A full glass of water per hour awake is recommended.)

- When learning the stretches, consult a more experienced KSS® user for proper form and execution, rather than learn-ing the poses incorrectly.

- Follow your stretching with a cool-down period, includ-ing sustaining the end of the stretch to avoid tenderness or stiffness. If soreness or stiffness occurs despite performing a cool-down, reduce your movements and try the modified 'M' version of the stretch.

Kousouli® Spinal Stretches (KSS®)

Beginning your new KSS® stretching routine is simple! Just pick three stretches (out of the nine provided) to do once in the morning, once in the afternoon, and once in the evening. They can be the same three stretches, but it is recommend that you mix it up in order to take full advantage of this process. Make sure you that you're paying special attention to your form, and giving these stretches the respect they deserve. They will change your life!

Please note: each stretch can be modified to your individual abilities! There will be a letter "M" next to suggested changes, but feel free to adapt your own until you become stronger or more adept at the stretches.

(A.) HERMES STRETCH

HERMES 1

HERMES 2

HERMES M1

HERMES M2

The Hermes stretch starts on your knees, and then you raise your opposite arm and feet in the air, pointing them as if you can fly. Start with one arm extended straight up over your shoulder and the knee bent towards your chest. Inhale deeply, and slightly extend your back as you hold the stretch for three seconds. Slowly switch the arms and legs as you exhale. Repeat the stretch on the opposite side. Modified Hermes is done lying on your back. This tones your core and helps burn body fat.

(B.) POSEIDON STRETCH

The Poseidon stretch starts with a crouched position, moving into a springing chest expansion. Crouch on the floor, inhale deeply from your diaphragm and rise up into a standing position with one leg back while extending the spine and pushing the chest out. Keep your arms wide, and hold up your chin. Hold for three seconds, and then exhale as you come back down into a crouched position. Repeat the stretch with the opposite leg. The modified version is staying seated while pushing your arms and chest out. This also tones your core, and stretches muscles we tend to overuse in the course of a workday.

(C.) EROS STRETCH

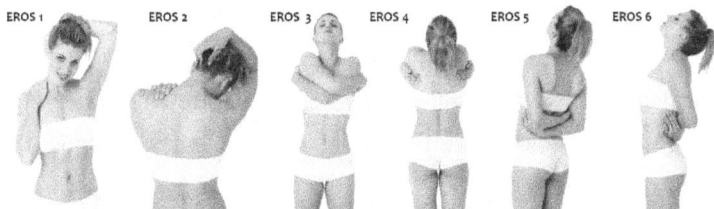

The Eros stretch requires you to stand with your left hand on your trapezius and pull the shoulder muscles down and forward. Anchor your fingers from your right hand onto the left posterior inferior occipital ridge (bottom left edge of skull, see picture: Eros2). Gently pull your head forward, down, and to the right with the chin towards your right chest. Inhale and exhale feeling the stretch. Repeat on the opposite side (Eros 1). Next, perform a loving heart hug by wrapping your arms around your chest (Eros 3, 4) as you extend your head back. With a gentle squeeze, try to move your fingers as far back to your spine as possible. Next, wrap your arms around your low back for support. Extend your upper body back gently, feeling the stretch (Eros 5, 6). The modified version of this stretch can be done seated. This stretch releases feel-good endorphins, and stretches muscles that retain stress.

(D.) APOLLO STRETCH

The Apollo is a great stretch to engage your muscles by starting in a standing position. Inhale deeply from your diaphragm, arch your spine, and push out your chest as you pull one arm and leg back. Put yourself into an archer position, and hold for a three second count. Exhale as you come back to starting position. Focus on the fluid motion of your body as tension builds upon extension of the back and arms. Repeat on the opposite side. Modify this stretch by kneeling or sitting with legs crossed. This engages the full body and invigorates you.

(E.) HEPHAESTUS STRETCH

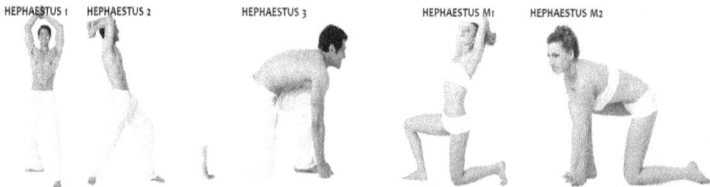

To do the Hephaestus stretch, move from an extended standing position to a crouched forward pose, as if you were wielding a large axe or hammer to the ground. Inhale as you slowly extend a leg and stretch back, hold for three seconds, and then come down gently forward overhead, bending the knees as you exhale. Rotate slightly your upper body through the movement to isolate the abdominals. Go slow and do not overextend your back. Repeat the stretch on the opposite side. Modified version is done by kneeling or sitting with legs crossed. This gets the whole body moving, and burns calories easily.

(F.) ATHENA STRETCH

To do this stretch, stand with flexed biceps as if you are holding a large shield in each arm. Extend slightly your spine and inhale deeply. Turn your arms and upper torso to one side and bring up the opposite knee. Tighten your abdominal muscles and hold for three seconds. Exhale and repeat on the other side. As you breathe deep from your diaphragm, perceive yourself as an impenetrable fortress. This core stretch will help you melt that belly fat off, and improve balance.

(G.) ZEUS STRETCH

This stretch should be started with your body crouched and then slowly extend your arms up as you stand into a body X position. Inhale deeply as you slowly stretch to the sky pushing up on your toes. Feel the stretch as you hold for three seconds. Exhale slowly as you descend back into a crouched position. As you descend and exhale, cross your arms as if throwing lightning bolts down to earth from the heavens. Repeat. Focus on the slow fluid motion of your body as tension builds up on the upward motion, and then releases on the downward flow. Modified Zeus stretch can be done kneeling or sitting with legs crossed. This burns calories and stretches nearly every muscle in your body, invigorating you.

(H.) DIONYSUS STRETCH

DIONYSUS 1  DIONYSUS 2  DIONYSUS M1  DIONYSUS M2

The Dionysus stretch is done standing in a saddle stance. Slowly bring up both arms as if holding an oversized glass of wine. Inhale deeply from your diaphragm, and slowly extend your torso as you rotate to one side. Gently extend your neck and upper back as if you are drinking the wine. Hold for three seconds, and keep your core tight. Return to center as you exhale, and then repeat on the opposite side. Your core, legs, arms, and neck are engaged, and the stretch feels great!

(I.) DEMETER STRETCH

DEMETER 1

DEMETER 2

DEMETER M1

DEMETER M2

For this stretch, lie on your back and inhale as you squeeze your knees to your chest; this signifies fertility or pregnancy (new life). Hold for three seconds, and then exhale as you slowly extend your legs down; depicting the seasonal summer/winter cycles. At the completion, slightly arch your cervical (neck) and the lumbar area (low back). Repeat. The modified version is done with hands palms down under the low back or hips for support, and makes the stretch a little easier. This stretch is very calming, and engages muscles that you may not use often in the lower body.

Benefits to the KSS® Stretch Program

KSS® combines a very unique mix of visual meditation, deep breathing and spinal exercise to provide an extremely powerful physical, mental, and spiritual exercise. All of the stretches are designed to improve your physical condition, which not only improves your health, but also improves your waistline. Each stretch is also a form of meditation, embracing your inner nature and helping you align your chi. When the mind, body, and spirit work together as they do in these exercises, you will not only feel and look better, but your energy will reach higher levels and you will be able to engage positively with yourself in order to live a healthier life.

Dr. Kousouli's Secret Fit Tip #31
30 MINUTES OF AEROBIC EXERCISE DAILY

Don't make the mistake of thinking that the stretches in this chapter are the end all. They are great for starting your daily body movement, but you should use them to transition into aerobic exercise. Many studies show that you actually need cardio (aerobic) exercise because your body doesn't enter fat-burning mode until your heart rate goes up. The ideal rate for each person varies, so talk to a doctor and trainer about your ideal aerobic heart rate.

My good friend Frank Tortorici, world-class fitness trainer and certified functional diagnostic nutritionist, says, "Consumers must pay attention to the food ingredients. You cannot out-exercise a poor diet and poor lifestyle. People have this concept that if they go on the treadmill for an hour they will burn off the calories, eliminating that horrible meal and dessert they had for dinner the night before. It's one of the most common mistakes I see."

So although exercise is very important, it's really about both adequate exercise and living a clean lifestyle. Make sure to incorporate everything you learned in this book and keep active! Add the KSS® to your daily regimen, join a gym, get a qualified trainer, do an aerobic exercise program, and after each workout, reward yourself with adequate hydration and hit the sauna for deep relaxation.

Dr. Kousouli's Secret Fit Tip #32
TAKE MORNING JOGS AND EVENING WALKS

A 2011 study published by Appalachian State University found that people who took morning jogs (or brisk walks) were actually less inclined to depression, had better overall heart health, and lived longer than people who didn't. In the same study, they found that people who took calm evening walks actually slept better, were thinner (because they burned their dinner calories before bed), and were calmer and less stressed.

Many other studies have discovered similar findings, and many of my patients tell me they feel their best when they are active first thing in the morning. There is something about being outside that helps too, and many studies have shown that being outside increases endorphins and all the feel-good chemicals (like dopamine) that make us happy. So create a new morning routine: Get up, get out, and go for a brisk walk or jog. Make a new routine for the evenings as well, and go out for a walk by yourself or with the family instead of sitting in front of the TV or computer all day! Your waistline and your energy will thank you for it.

Chapter Eleven:
Adding Supplements to Support Weight Loss

"Some things you have to do every day. Eating seven apples
on Saturday night instead of one a day just isn't
going to get the job done."

~ *Jim Rohn*

Now that you've established what you need to cut out, change, and add to your daily life in order to get "Hollywood skinny," you're probably ready to rock. Once you've established a balanced diet and a great exercise routine, you're going to notice the pounds begin to melt away. But what do we do to help our bodies and support them through this change (and through life in general)? I recommend finding all-natural supplements that boost your body's performance.

There is a difference between all-natural supplements and weight loss supplements or diet pills. I am *not* advocating that you buy anything that claims to "Help you lose weight fast!" I am only sharing my opinions on smart science, healthy supplements, and even better ways to boost your health. Supplements should do exactly that - supplement - <u>not</u> replace healthy whole foods and nutrition. Use them <u>after</u> you do everything else.

But even with proper diet and exercise, some of us can have deficiencies in certain minerals and vitamins. Other times, we expend so much energy exercising that we need to help our body replace what it burns off. Other recommendations I have listed below help your body enter an alkaline state, and can help you increase your gut health – all of which we have discussed in previous chapters.

Dr. Kousouli's Secret Fit Tip #33
TRY NATURAL SUPPLEMENTS FOR WEIGHT LOSS

Disclaimer: **Please note that side effects may exist with natural herbs. Proper care is needed for correct administration and use.** Everyone's situation is different. Do not mix supplements or herbs with medications you are already taking, without first checking with your primary health care provider(s) for your specific needs. Some herbs should not be taken by those with certain diseases, or by women who are pregnant or nursing. The following information is provided to you for educational purposes only, and as a general synopsis of possible options that should be discussed with your doctor(s). All readers should consult their own appropriate health professionals for more information, instruction, dosage, and any other matter relating to their personal health and well-being. The information has not been evaluated or approved by the Food and Drug Administration for the treatment or cure of any disease, disorder, syndrome, or ailment mentioned herein. Reader uses this and all information herein at their own risk.

- *Green Coffee Bean Extract:* Contains chlorogenic acid, which inhibits the release of glucose and increases the metabolic liver process to help shed pounds. The caffeine present also helps boost metabolism. Ask a doctor first if you are diabetic or on medications.

- *Garcinia Cambogia Extract:* Increases serotonin and blocks the enzymes your brain sends out to make fat. Overall, decreased hunger and higher satiety occurs so you eat less. May help decrease blood sugar and bad levels of cholesterol.

- *Conjugated Linoleic Acid (CLA):* Decreases body fat in adults; believed to reduce feelings of hunger. Note: ask your holistic professionals about taking this if you have diabetes.

- *Chromium Picolinate:* Works with insulin to transfer carbs into energy. Believed to lower cholesterol and help with weight loss because it transfers sugar into energy rather than fat.

- *Glucomannan:* Water-soluble fiber used in supplements and weight loss drink mixes. It helps fill up your stomach and makes you feel fuller longer with few calories. Try to find meal replacement shakes that have this, or get the powdered version to make your own drinks.

- *Guarana:* High in caffeine - nearly double what coffee offers. This can help boost your energy in the morning and after a workout, and increase metabolism.

- *Guar Gum:* Helps with digestion, and is a water-soluble fiber. Especially helpful with digestive issues like chronic constipation, Crohn's disease, etc. May decrease cholesterol and high blood pressure.

- *Ginseng:* Boosts immunity, decreases inflammatory conditions in the body. Improves memory, immune system function, heart and brain health. Careful with higher dosage, check with your doctor.

- *Hydroxycitric Acid (HCA):* Believed to burn visceral fat. Some studies show that it reduces weight, cholesterol, and food cravings. Check with your doctor.

- *Beta Glucan:* Water-soluble fiber that promotes slower digestion. Reduced cholesterol, body fat, risk of diabetes, and improved metabolism result.

- *Mango Seed Fiber:* Shows significant promise in addressing weight loss. Improves blood sugar, cholesterol, and hormones that trigger hunger response.

- *Bitter Orange:* Used in treating constipation, indigestion, heartburn, and may promote weight loss.

- **Fucoxanthin:** Fat-burning carotenoid found in wakame and red seaweed. Also considered an anti-inflammatory and shows promising results as an anti-cancer supplement.

- **Chitosan:** Disrupts lipid uptake and blocks body's response to hunger. Also shows promise for indigestion, Crohn's disease, etc. Decreases cholesterol.

- **Dehydroepiandrosterone (DHEA):** An adrenal steroid hormone; may help body fat reduction.

- **Hoodia Gordonii:** Popular natural weight loss herb from a South African succulent plant; used for centuries to suppress appetite.

- **Liquid Chlorophyll and Chlorella:** Helps alkalize the blood stream and neutralize toxins. Add to your water or food; several drops with every glass or meal.

For more thorough information on how to naturally help over 60 diseases common in America, check out *BE A MASTER® OF MAXIMUM HEALING*. Talk to your holistic health professionals about what they recommend, and only take what makes sense for your life, health, and body.

Chapter Twelve:
Conclusion

"The answers to life and the universe are simple; their secrets
freely given to all at the very end."
~ Dr. Theo Kousouli

I hope the 'real life' information in this book has helped you look at your health and well-being from a new found perspective. It's imperative that we look at weight loss and overall body image by taking a step back, remove all the glam and glitz from the marketing industry, and take action on the things that actually give us solutions. Go ahead and research the topics discussed, you will find that they sit sound in years of scientific research. There's no hocus-pocus or magic pills here. Yes, you will have to challenge yourself and put a little bit of effort into it, but now you have the necessary ammunition for an honest shot at success!

While nobody can say exactly what you need to do to be happy and healthy in your own skin, I do know that it starts with a simple decision. Decide to work towards your weight loss goals, decide to choose healthy paths rather than fast, easy, or chemically laden ones, and decide to become the YOU you want to be. We were all made in God's image, and He doesn't make mistakes. It's up to us, the human form of creation to decide how we shape our divinity. Remember this every time you hit a road bump, every time you struggle to fit in that workout or make that healthy food choice. Your Creator is in your corner, and He/She/It is helping you become the person you are meant to be with every choice you make.

The advice given in this book should not be taken as a "one size fits all" approach. Please be sure to see your doctor for proper diagnosis and management and, as always, use your judgment and personal history as a filter for this information. Only you and your doctor(s) know what is best for you, but I hope the information provided in this book helps you make your path to greatness easier. You can do it!

See you at the seminars!

In the highest vibration of love and light -

God bless,

Theodoros Kousouli D.C., CHt.

About the Author

A holistic health care advisor, teacher, speaker, mentor and author who is featured on major networks, Theodoros Kousouli D.C., CHt., is Los Angeles' premier holistic metaphysical energy healer. He is recognized and trusted for effective, quick, drug-free results. His remarkable natural, pain-free, holistic healing system - the Kousouli® Method - focuses on getting patients to their top performance levels by unblocking pathways using the body's own repair mechanisms.

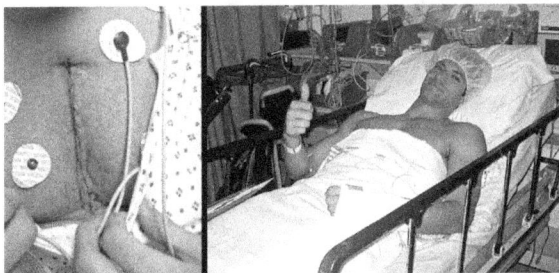

His desire to help others stems from his personal journey recovering from semi-paralysis and major heart surgeries, and includes everything he's learned about the optimum wellness techniques that define his practice.

Dr. Theo Kousouli is the author of seven previous books, including: *BE A MASTER® of PSYCHIC ENERGY and BE A MASTER® of MAXIMUM HEALING*. A personal coach and advisor to entertainers, business leaders, energy healers, and spiritual seekers of all varieties, Dr. Kousouli holds seminars teaching people how to tap into their inner healing and higher-level abilities through the use of their nervous systems. Visit **www.KousouliMethod.com** for more information on developing your intuition and personal power to live a more purpose-filled, meaningful, and healthy life. Dr. Kousouli is the ideal speaker for your next event.

To Schedule Dr. Theo Kousouli For Your Next Event:

www.DrKousouli.com

Be a Master® of Self Image

BE A MASTER® OF MAXIMUM HEALING
How to Lead a Healthy Life Without Limits

• Holistics Solutions for over 60 Diseases to Help You and Your Loved Ones Heal!

BE A MASTER® OF PSYCHIC ENERGY
Your Key to Truly Mastering Your Personal Power

• Uncover and Amplify Your Hidden Psychic Abilities to Change Your Life!

BE A MASTER® OF SEX ENERGY
Hypnotize Your Partner for Love and Great Sex

• Build a Stronger Bond with Your Lover(s) Using Subconcious Science!

BE A MASTER® OF SUCCESS
Dr.Kousouli's 33 Master Secrets to Achieving Your Dreams

• Solid Success Principles You can Apply to Empower Your Life!

BE A MASTER® OF SELF LOVE
Dr.Kousouli's 33 Master Secrets to Loving Your Extraordinary Life

• Overcome Bullying, Abuse, Depression and Build Massive Self-Esteem & Self-Love!

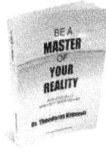

BE A MASTER® OF YOUR REALITY
Authentically Manifest Your Desires

• Use the Law of Attraction to Radically Transform Your Life!

If you would like to share your story of how Dr. Kousouli's books, audios or seminars have impacted your life for the better, we would love to hear from you! (Messages are screened by staff and forwarded when appropriate.)

For A Free Gift from Dr. Theo Kousouli visit www.FreeGiftFromDrTheo.com

www.ingramcontent.com/pod-product-compliance
Lightning Source LLC
LaVergne TN
LVHW021542080426
835509LV00019B/2798